THIS BOOK BELONGS TO:

Let's Learn Our Way Through It, Shall We?

DAILY JOURNALING:

Learn Something New Every Day

Ekpedeme "Pamay" M. Bassey

Book Cover Design: Kerry LaCoste
Interior Design: LaCoste Design Co., Inc.
Illustrations: iStockphoto and DepositPhotos
Photography: Getty Images, Pexels and iStockphoto
Edited by Jenny Sullivan

To my mother,

Dr. Patricia M. Bassey

~~~~~~

Thank you for moving heaven and earth
to ensure that The Bassey Girls could have access
to the best education possible—
and for teaching us that the only things
that can never be taken away from us are the
things that we learn. Love you, Ma!

~~~~~~

And to my friends, family, and colleagues.
Thank you for teaching me something new
every single day.

to learn

IS TO GROW

Let life inspire and teach you
every day of the year.

to reflect

IS TO REMEMBER

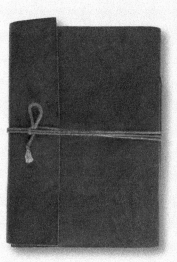

An elephant may never forget, but
sometimes we do. Reflecting on what you learned,
and writing the ideas and inspiration
that you take from the learning experiences
you have will help you to remember,
as will taking the time to apply those lessons
in your every day life.

Contents

TABLE OF CONTENTS

Embrace

the Value Proposition

~~~~~~

At the end of 2018, I found myself beginning an exciting new position as Chief Learning Officer of the Kraft Heinz Company. In many ways, it was a dream job. Having been in learning and development for more than 20 years, I was to be responsible for creating a culture of continuous learning, bold creativity, and intellectual curiosity, for driving training and learning initiatives at one of the largest food companies in the world. It was a great challenge.

When you are called to take on a new challenge, it is wise to gather the lessons learned from prior experience and see how they can be applied. I drew from my passion project, the *My 52 Weeks of Worship*

Project, which started when I made a personal commitment to visit a different place of worship every week for a year. That project turned into a book, *My 52 Weeks of Worship: Lessons from a Global, Spiritual, Interfaith Journey*, and a TEDx talk, *Navigating Sacred Spaces*.

Inspired by the lessons learned from my passion project, and by the challenge ahead, I launched *My 365 Days of Learning* on a snowy day in Canada, during a ride from a leadership retreat to the Toronto airport, heading home to Chicago. This second year-long learning experience of mine also started with a personal commitment, but was focused on delivering professional impact. This time, instead of a weekly commitment, I would make a daily commitment. I made a promise: every day for a year, I would learn something new, and would share it with the organization through our internal social media channel.

I was able to model how leaders could be lifelong learners: to #MakeTimeForLearning. This was a "must" for a learning leader of a large, global enterprise to show others the benefits of a learning practice and encourage them. Sometimes my daily learning moment was just a few minutes long; occasionally, it was a few hours. I consumed articles, eLearning courses, podcasts, and books. I attended conferences and learning events. I spent time each day writing, reflecting on what I had learned, and sharing it with others. Most excitingly, I watched my new colleagues do the same, committing to a learning practice of their own and creating a culture of generosity—because by learning, and reflecting and sharing, they were empowering others as well as themselves. *My 365 Days of Learning* became the foundation of a learning transformation for a company going through significant change. A vibrant learning culture is an important ingredient to fuel any organizational transformation, and it was exciting to see progress being made in creating that culture. On February 1, 2020, I celebrated the completion of 365 consecutive days of learning.

My year of learning started with the creation of a value proposition statement for Learning and Development. It stated that our learning and development offerings enabled each employee to learn like an owner so they could execute with excellence in their current roles, accelerate their learning curve, and grow great careers. That value proposition was a contract between learners and my team. We expected learners to take ownership of their learning and development, knowing that the benefit would come to them as a result.

As you hold this journal in your hand, about to start your own learning journey, I invite you to embrace that value proposition for yourself. Transform yourself and others into lifelong learners. If you want to create a powerful and functional learning culture, and embrace your role as catalyst—in your life, in the lives of your family, in your community, or in your organization—I invite you to consider the Seven Steps of Learning Transformation, which I also will share throughout this journal. Step 1 of those seven steps is to *Embrace The Value Proposition*.

During my year of learning, I wrote a list of "365 Things I Learned from 365 Days of Learning," and I share those 365 things in this journal. Use them as inspiration to reflect on and write about what *you* are learning—what you need to learn—from your day, and from whatever formal or informal learning experience you are having each day.

Don't worry if it's not the beginning of a calendar year. As you flip to page 1, you will see the lesson: "It sure feels good to make a promise to yourself and keep it." Making that promise can happen at any time. Start your year today—whether it is the beginning of a week, a month, or a year. Maybe you need to revisit some of the promises you made at the beginning of this new year about how this year would be different than previous years. Maybe your last year was so disrupted by unforeseen events that you need to take a moment to breathe, remember who you said you wanted to be, and start on the path to becoming that person. It's never too late to reboot your year if you need to get on track with your resolutions and intentions.

There is power in making a commitment to be a lifelong learner. There is power in making a commitment to start a new habit—even if you start with a few minutes a day. There is power in deciding to be the Chief Learning Officer of your life as you continue to work toward the best version of yourself.

Welcome to the next 365 days of your life. Let's learn our way through it, shall we?

Pamay

Commit

Commit

to #LearnLikeAnOwner

After you *Embrace the Value Proposition*, Step 2 in the Seven Steps of Learning Transformation is to *Commit to #LearnLikeAnOwner*. And what does *#LearnLikeAnOwner* mean? It means three things. As you take responsibility for your own learning and development:

1. Seek out high-impact learning experiences.
2. Commit to a learning practice, even if it is just a few minutes a day, and
3. Encourage others to do the same.

That's it—simple, but not easy.

You may be wondering: how should I use *this* journal as I Commit to #LearnLikeAnOwner? Well, here are some suggestions:

In this journal, I share 365 lessons that I gathered during *My 365 Days of Learning*. *One way to use the journal is to think about each of the lessons that I share, one day at a time, and write your reaction to it.* What did the lesson bring up in your mind? Is it relevant to a challenge that you are currently grappling with? Might it inspire you to do something differently? Whatever the answer is - simply write it in the journal.

Periodically, at the bottom of a page, you will see a question to prompt your thinking. Where I have not provided a question prompt, think of your own. Get in the habit of questioning the things you learn so you can determine what is useful to you, and what is not. I invite you to consider the many lessons I learned during my year of learning and use them as motivation for your own learning journey.

Another way to use this journal is to start your own learning journey immediately. Decide, for 30 days, to commit to learning something new every day. Flip to the back of the journal and, in the empty pages, jot down the lessons you learn along the way.

If you are wondering what kind of learning commitment to make, my suggestion is: let your curiosity guide you. Don't worry about restricting yourself to certain types of learning – or about how long your learning experience each day is—it could be listening to a 15-minute podcast or choosing to practice a key communication skill during a difficult conversation.

Frequently, when I talk to people about what it means to #Learn-LikeAnOwner, they ask me, "If I make a commitment to learn something every day, what counts as learning?" And "If I make a commitment to #MakeTimeForLearning, how much time do I need to spend so that it counts?" The answer: it all counts. Every learning experience counts. Every minute counts.

However you decide to use the journal – and you really can use it any way you want - know that the point is to commit to creating a learning habit. Learn, reflect, and share what you learned. Be consistent. Consistency is important if you want to make a habit stick.

Simply focus on thinking of yourself as a learner, as someone who can learn your way through anything. Ready?

Let's go!

1.

IT SURE FEELS GOOD TO MAKE A PROMISE TO YOURSELF
AND KEEP IT.

....

....

....

....

....

....

....

....

....

....

....

....

Have you made a promise to learn something new
every day, reflect upon it, and share it with others?
If not, what is holding you back?

2.

START BEFORE YOU ARE READY.

....

....

....

....

....

....

....

3.

DOING SOMETHING EVERY DAY FOR 365 DAYS IS
DIFFICULT AND AWESOME.

....

....

....

....

....

....

....

4.

IT IS OKAY TO MAKE A QUIET COMMITMENT. Sometimes it turns into a movement, sometimes it doesn't. But regardless of how public the commitment, small consistent actions can be transformational.

....

....

....

....

....

....

....

....

....

....

....

....

....

....

5.

BRING YOUR WHOLE SELF TO
THE CHALLENGE. EVERY TIME.

....

....

....

....

....

....

....

....

....

....

....

If we are self-aware, we know our own roadblocks – the things
that prevent us from keeping promises to ourselves. What,
if anything, stands in the way of you being your best self?

6.

EMBRACING YOUR CONSTRAINTS CAN UNLEASH CREATIVITY.

....

....

....

....

....

....

....

....

....

....

....

....

....

Constraints are a gift. What constraints are you facing that can inspire your creativity?

7.

NO MATTER WHAT YOU ARE WORKING ON, IF YOU ASK
YOURSELF "WHO NEEDS TO KNOW," YOU CAN BRING PEOPLE
ALONG ON THE JOURNEY.

....

....

....

....

....

....

8.

COMMUNICATION + COLLABORATION = POWER.

....

....

....

....

....

....

....

9.

SOMETIMES IT'S SMART TO GET REALLY STUPID. Sometimes when you need to learn something new, it's smart to "get stupid" — humble yourself and start from the beginning.

....

....

....

....

....

....

....

....

....

....

....

....

....

....

....

10.

RESILIENCE, AND LEARNING HOW TO DEVELOP IT,
CAN MAKE ALL THE DIFFERENCE.

....

....

....

....

....

....

11.

BE PRESENT.

....

....

....

....

....

....

....

12.

LEARNING SOME THINGS WILL JUST BE PAINFUL,
SO BUCKLE YOUR SEATBELT.

....

....

....

....

....

....

....

....

....

....

....

....

....

What difficult thing are you tackling today?

13.

TAKING CHARGE OF YOUR OWN LEARNING AND
DEVELOPMENT CAN BE THE GIFT THAT KEEPS ON GIVING.

....

....

....

....

....

....

14.

EMBRACE THE SUCCESS CYCLE: TRY, FAIL, LEARN, SUCCEED.
REPEAT AS MANY TIMES AS IT TAKES.

....

....

....

....

....

....

15.

THE FIRST FEW DAYS OF ANYTHING SETS THE TONE FOR
YOUR SUCCESS OR STRUGGLE.

....

....

....

....

....

....

....

....

....

....

....

....

Whether it is starting a new habit, a new job, or a
new role, what can you do to start strong?

16.

THERE IS NOTHING IN THE WORLD AS POWERFUL
AS COMMITMENT.

....

....

....

....

....

....

....

....

....

....

....

....

....

If you have made it to 16 days in a row of writing in this
journal, does it feel awesome? If you haven't – what will
it take to recommit to your learning journey?

17.

NO MATTER WHAT THE STORM, YOU CAN
LEARN YOUR WAY THROUGH IT.

18.

MINDSET IS EVERYTHING.

....

....

....

....

....

....

....

....

....

....

....

> If you haven't read Carol Dweck's book, Mindset:
> The New Psychology of Success, you should.
> Decide to focus on developing a growth mindset
> as you become a continuous learner.

19.

TAKING THE TIME TO REFLECT HELPS YOU TO APPLY YOUR LEARNING IN DIFFERENT CONTEXTS. "Learn, Reflect, Share, Practice." As you learn different things, share what you learned.

20.

CALCULATING YOUR RETURN ON FAILURE
CAN HELP YOU TO FAIL FORWARD.

....

....

....

....

....

....

....

21.

THERE IS POWER IN TURNING A VICTIM MINDSET
INTO AN EMPOWER MINDSET.

....

....

....

....

....

....

....

22.

EVERYONE SHOULD KNOW THEIR EINSTEIN WINDOW.

....

....

....

....

....

....

....

....

....

....

....

....

....

Your Einstein window is the time during the day when you are at your mental peak. What are the hours in the day when you are most effective? Discover your Einstein window and protect it for the most important tasks of your day.

23.

IF SOMETHING IS TOO BIG TO LEARN
ALL IN ONE SITTING, CHOP IT UP.

....

....

....

....

....

....

24.

IF YOU ARE FACING A CHALLENGE, LEARN YOUR WAY
THROUGH IT.

....

....

....

....

....

....

25.

EACH FAILURE IS AN OPPORTUNITY TO LEARN AND GROW.

....

....

....

....

....

....

....

....

....

....

....

....

Think back over the past year. Is there something that you tried that didn't end up quite the way that you planned? What, if anything, did you learn from that thing?

26.

DON'T MISTAKE MOTION FOR MEANING.

....
....
....
....
....
....
....
....
....
....
....
....
....
....

What are you doing that you can stop doing so you can make the best use of your time to do what really matters?

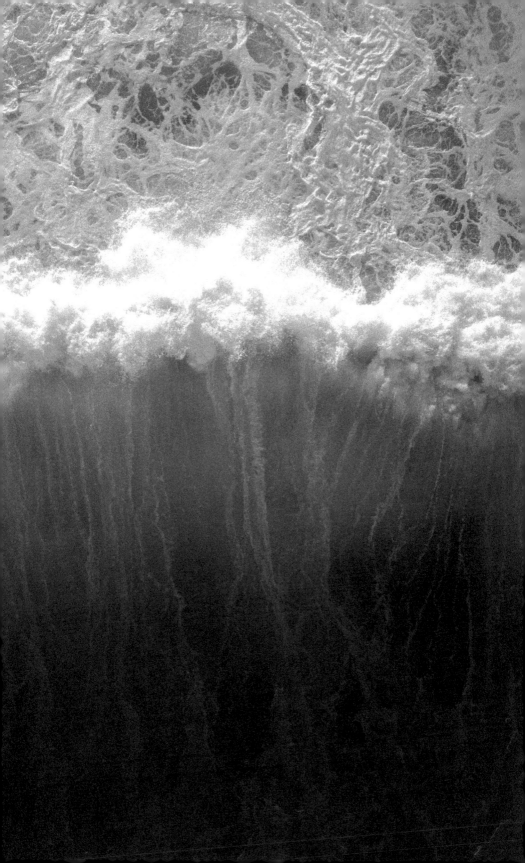

27.

MAKE SELF-DEVELOPMENT FUN.

....

....

....

....

....

....

....

....

....

....

....

....

Research shows that there is a connection between laughter and learning. What skill do you need to develop? How can you make it more fun?

28.

DO IT NOW. Creating a practice of "doing it now" can possibly be the most powerful practice of all. Plans are pointless unless they include direct action to reach the end goal.

....

....

....

....

....

....

....

....

....

....

....

....

....

....

....

29.

IF YOU THINK YOU KNOW SOMETHING, BUT YOU CAN'T REALLY EXPLAIN IT TO SOMEONE ELSE, YOU DON'T REALLY KNOW IT.

....

....

....

....

....

....

....

....

....

....

....

Choosing to teach back is powerful. In sharing and teaching what you know, you can deepen your knowledge. What do you know that you can teach others?

30.

SOMETIMES YOU NEED TO STEP BACK TO GROW.

....

....

....

....

....

....

....

....

....

....

....

....

....

Whitney Johnson, the world's leading expert on
personal disruption, taught me this and so much more.
If you don't know her work, you should make a point
to familiarize yourself with it.

31.

BE OPEN TO LEARNING FROM UNEXPECTED PEOPLE, PLACES, AND THINGS.

Gather

Gather

the Lessons as You Unleash Your Superpower

LESSONS 32-363

You made it through the first 31 days! Congratulations! So glad you have decided to embrace the value proposition and that you made the commitment to #LearnLikeAnOwner.

Now, you will continue to travel the road of your personal learning journey — considering the lessons that I learned and gathering your own. Get ready to experience Step 3 through Step 6 of the Seven Steps of Learning Transformation:

Step 3: Determine your searching and learning style
How? Use your life. The things that are happening in your life should be your motivation for the topics, skills and capabilities on which you focus your learning time. Are you an exploratory learner? A search bar can be a great tool to find interesting articles, podcasts, and other learning materials. Do you prefer to find a playlist or a curriculum that can guide you? Then spend some time during your learning journey searching for just the right one.

Step 4: Identify your trusted sources of learning

Continue to ask yourself: how do I like to absorb information? What and who are my trusted sources of learning? Are there specific business or thought leaders that I admire? Individuals from totally different walks of life who inspire me? Scholarly journals or publications that always challenge me? As you consume information from different sources of learning, develop a list of trusted go-to sources. They will serve you and streamline your learning searches over time.

Step 5: Reflect on and share what you are learning

Reflection helps you apply your learning in different contexts. The time you take to pause, think about what you learned and how it can be applied in the context of your unique challenges is almost as valuable as the time spent learning itself.

Step 6: Determine what to practice and what to keep

It is through practice that we move from simply being aware of something, to being able to apply it. Practice makes permanent. Over time, you will see what works for you, and what doesn't: keep what works and discard the rest.

Most importantly – have fun! There are no rules to this thing. If you are flipping through the lessons and are more inspired by one lesson than another – even if you are not going in order-that's okay! Contemplate each lesson as you take your own learning journey, keep your learning commitment, and unleash your learning superpower. Write about the things you have learned, and what you plan to practice. Later, reflect on those things.

Ready? Let's go!

32.

BE AN INFINITE LEARNER.

....

....

....

....

....

....

....

33.

SOME USEFUL QUESTIONS TO ASK AT ANY TIME: "WHO IS GOING TO DO WHAT, WHEN…AND WHY IS THAT GOING TO HAPPEN?"

....

....

....

....

....

34.

THERE IS A FAIR AMOUNT OF DISCUSSION ABOUT THE
BEST WAY TO LEAD OTHERS, BUT IT IS WISE ALSO TO FIGURE
OUT HOW TO LEAD YOURSELF.

....

....

....

....

....

....

....

....

....

....

....

What is the most difficult thing for you to commit to
doing regularly? How can you turn that challenge into
consistent right action?

35.

HIGH-GROWTH ORGANIZATIONS NEED HIGH-GROWTH INDIVIDUALS.

....

....

....

....

....

....

....

36.

YOUR JOB AS A LEADER IS TO SCALE EXCELLENCE.

....

....

....

....

....

....

....

37.

MY DAD HAD A SIGN IN HIS OFFICE FOR YEARS THAT SAID, "THE BUCK STOPS HERE."
He and Harry S. Truman were on to something.

....

....

....

....

....

....

....

....

....

....

My father, Dr. Ephraim N. Bassey was one of the smartest people I ever knew. Sometimes you can draw inspiration from the great learners in your life. Who are they? Identify them and talk to them. Chances are they can teach you a great deal.

38.

AS THOUGHT LEADER WHITNEY JOHNSON SAYS, "PERIODICALLY, DISRUPT YOURSELF." Take the right risks, play to your distinctive strengths, embrace constraints, battle entitlement, step back to grow, give failure its due, and be discovery driven.

....

....

....

....

....

....

....

....

....

....

....

....

....

....

39.

I'D MUCH RATHER READ A BOOK THAN LISTEN TO
SOMEONE TALK TO ME ABOUT A BOOK.

....

....

....

....

....

....

....

....

....

....

....

....

Knowing your learning style is essential. I like reading
books more than listening to book summaries, but
that's me. What are your trusted sources of learning?

40.

YOU CAN LEARN A LOT FROM SURFERS.

....
....
....
....
....
....
....
....
....
....
....
....

Learning comes from where it comes from, even if
you don't have any experience with the source or the
context. In what unexpected places can you find lessons
that can help you in your life?

41.

PRACTICE. PRACTICE. PRACTICE.

....

....

....

....

....

....

....

....

....

....

....

....

....

....

....

42.

IF YOUR INTENTION IS TO HARNESS COLLECTIVE WISDOM,
MAKE SURE YOU ARE DOING IT.

....

....

....

....

....

....

....

....

....

....

....

....

....

Decision making can be challenging; make sure you are
using all the tools at your disposal when you must
make an important decision. Whose counsel can you
seek about a decision that you are making today?

43.

LEADERS UNDERESTIMATE THE WORK A TEAM IS
DOING BY 50%.

....

....

....

....

....

....

....

....

....

....

....

Are you overburdening yourself or your team because
you are not accurately counting the amount of work
being done? What can you do better? Can you ask
questions, listen, and right-size the load so you can
optimize output?

44.

IF YOU FIND THAT YOU ARE STUCK, ASK YOURSELF, "AM I ADDRESSING THE RIGHT CONCERN? AM I ANSWERING THE RIGHT QUESTION?" Always ask yourself: What is the right problem? Then solve that problem.

....

....

....

....

....

....

....

....

....

....

....

....

....

....

....

....

45.

FOCUS ON DEEP WORK. MAKE TIME FOR
WORK THAT MATTERS.

....

....

....

....

....

....

46.

LISTENING IS A LEADERSHIP PRACTICE.

....

....

....

....

....

....

47.

CONSIDER THE LOSADA RATIO.

....

....

....

....

....

....

....

....

....

....

....

The Losada Ratio is, "The sum of the positivity in a system divided by the sum of its negativity." Use it as you consider the type of feedback you are giving yourself or your team. Are you being intentional about the amount of positive feedback you are giving in comparison to the amount of negative feedback you are giving?

48.

BEING A LONE NUT CAN START A MOVEMENT. Being a first follower is a momentum-building gift.

....

....

....

....

....

....

....

....

....

....

....

....

If you haven't seen the "Leadership Lessons from a Dancing Guy" video or Derek Siver's TED talk on how to start a movement, make the time to do that. Then this lesson will make plenty of sense. Plus, the video is hilarious while being brilliantly instructive.

49.

WEIGH OPTIONS. MITIGATE RISKS. MANAGE BIAS.
MAKE GREAT DECISIONS.

....

....

....

....

....

....

....

....

....

....

....

....

Making informed decisions is a necessary and important skill. Is there a difficult decision that you need to make? How can you make sure you are managing your biases when you make it?

50.

CREATIVITY IS A SKILL, WHICH MEANS YOU CAN GET BETTER
AT IT OVER TIME IF YOU PRACTICE IT.

....

....

....

....

....

....

51.

BE A GENEROUS LEADER.

....

....

....

....

....

....

....

52.

DON'T BE A HIPPO. BE AN ELEPHANT.

....

....

....

....

....

....

....

....

....

....

....

....

Hippos have a big mouth and tiny ears. Elephants have a tiny mouth and huge ears. Often the best thing is to talk less and listen more. Where in your life can you apply this lesson?

53.

MAKE CULTURE A PRIORITY.

....

....

....

....

....

....

....

54.

BE A THOUSAND PERCENT CONVINCED IN YOUR OWN
HEAD, OR YOU WON'T GET ACROSS THE FINISH LINE.
Commitment is everything. It is especially useful when you
are doing a difficult thing.

....

....

....

....

....

....

55.

START-UP SOUL IS REAL.

....

....

....

....

....

....

....

....

....

....

....

There is an energy, a passion that exists in a start-up venture. It helps to neutralize the challenges that come when you are building something from scratch. How can you harness that type of energy or purpose in whatever project is important to you?

56.

NEVER STOP LEARNING HOW TO BE A POSITIVE LEADER.

....

....

....

....

....

....

57.

DREAM BIG.

....

....

....

....

....

....

58.

INCONSISTENT DECISION-MAKING CAN COST YOU.

....
....
....
....
....
....
....

59.

EXECUTIVE PRESENCE MAKES A DIFFERENCE.

....
....
....
....
....
....

60.

ELITE ATHLETES CAN TEACH US A LOT ABOUT
EMBRACING CHANGE.

....

....

....

....

....

....

....

61.

WE ARE ALL IMPROVISING. LEARN HOW TO DO IT WELL.

....

....

....

....

....

....

....

62.

BEHAVE WITH URGENCY EVERY DAY.

....

....

....

....

....

....

63.

LEARN FROM WHAT YOUR TEAM IS LEARNING.

....

....

....

....

....

....

64.

LEARN HOW TO BE INDISTRACTABLE.

....
....
....
....
....
....
....
....
....
....
....
....
....

Nir Eyal wrote a book called Indistractable: How to Control Your Attention and Choose Your Life. I highly recommend it. Where is your focus fractured? How can you fix it?

65.

TO BE SUCCESSFUL SOMEDAY, YOU MUST KNOW WHAT
YOUR PERSONAL DEFINITION OF SUCCESS IS.

....

....

....

....

....

....

....

66.

REACH OTHERS WITH EMPATHY, SIMPLICITY, AND CLARITY.

....

....

....

....

....

....

....

67.

TOMATOES ARE SO COOL.

....

....

....

....

....

....

....

....

....

One of my coolest learning experiences was traveling to Stockton, California, to visit a research farm where I learned about agriculture, seed operations, and tomato technology. During the visit, one of the farmers said, as he showed me the rows of tomato plants and pointed out which plants were likely to grow strong and which were not: "Deep roots yield good crops." Wise words. Where can you plant deep roots so you can yield good crops?

68.

A CLEAR COMPANY VISION CAN
BE POWERFUL.

....

....

....

....

....

....

....

69.

REMAIN HUMBLE EVEN AS YOU LEAD.

....

....

....

....

....

....

....

70.

YOU MAY NOT BE AS INFLUENTIAL AS YOU THINK.

....

....

....

....

....

....

....

....

....

....

....

....

Are you making the impact you would like to make?
Are you sure? Who can you ask for feedback so you
can be sure? What do you need to practice to become
more impactful?

71.

USE YOUR LIFE. The things that are happening in your day and in your life can and should be the motivation for the topics, skills, and capabilities on which you focus your learning time.

....

....

....

....

....

....

....

....

....

....

Has something challenging happened in your life recently? What do you need to learn to manage that situation effectively?

72.

IT TAKES SKILL TO PROVIDE STRUCTURE
THAT ISN'T STIFLING.

....

....

....

....

....

....

73.

GIVE PEOPLE A VOICE. REAP THE REWARD.

....

....

....

....

....

....

74.

IT'S NEVER A BAD IDEA TO KNOW WHAT IS ON
YOUR BOSS' MIND.

....

....

....

....

....

....

....

75.

LEARN HOW TO CREATE HABITS THAT WILL SUPPORT
YOUR SUCCESS.

....

....

....

....

....

....

....

76.

MAKE TIME TO LEAD. BE CLEAR ON WHAT "BEING BUSY" IS PREVENTING YOU FROM DOING THAT YOU REALLY SHOULD BE DOING.

....

....

....

....

....

....

77.

HABITS OFTEN BEAT NOVELTY.

....

....

....

....

....

....

....

78.

WHERE THERE IS A WHY, THERE IS A WAY.

....

....

....

....

....

....

....

....

....

....

....

Knowing what drives you, what matters, can be a powerful force to propel you to your good. What is your purpose? If you don't know, can you commit some time to asking yourself difficult questions so you can determine your why?

79.

LEARN. PRACTICE. REPEAT. It may take many times to learn something and practice it before you master it. Give yourself as much time as you need so that you can learn whatever it is you need to know.

....

....

....

....

....

....

....

....

....

....

....

....

....

....

....

80.

MAKE A POINT TO PRACTICE EVERYDAY COURAGE.

....

....

....

....

....

....

....

....

....

....

....

Life provides opportunities for us to practice being brave every day. Where can you choose to be courageous today? To be brave?

81.

YOU CAN'T SPEND ENOUGH TIME LEARNING HOW TO MANAGE STRESS.

....

....

....

....

....

....

....

....

....

....

....

During my year of learning, I used the word "stress" as a search term to find new learning materials and experiences many times. I even took the same LinkedIn Learning course twice from Todd Dewett on managing stress. Managing stress is a critical skill. How do you manage your stress?

82.

LEADERS DRIVE CULTURE. When those in charge are committed, things change.

....

....

....

....

....

....

83.

DON'T LET POWER CORRUPT YOU. As you increase your power and influence, staying anchored in your core values can be wise.

....

....

....

....

....

....

84.

INTEGRITY IS EVERYTHING. Determine how you will walk through the world and do your best to do that.

....
....
....
....
....
....

85.

TO BE AN EFFECTIVE LEADER, YOU MUST BE TRUSTWORTHY.

....
....
....
....
....
....

86.

OF ALL THE DIFFERENT KINDS OF LEADERSHIP, SERVANT LEADERSHIP IS AN APPROACH EVERYONE SHOULD CONSIDER.

....

....

....

....

....

....

....

....

....

....

....

....

Do you think that the goal of a leader is to serve?

87.

THERE IS TREMENDOUS POWER IN SIMPLY
ASKING THE RIGHT QUESTIONS.

....

....

....

....

....

....

88.

BEING RESPONSIBLE AND BEING ACCOUNTABLE ARE
NOT THE SAME THING.

....

....

....

....

....

....

89.

BEYOND BEING CONCERNED ABOUT MANAGING YOUR TIME,
BE CONCERNED ABOUT MANAGING YOUR ENERGY.

....

....

....

....

....

....

....

....

....

....

Tony Schwartz is a thought leader focused on the
importance of managing your energy. You may want
to research him. Ask yourself: am I managing my time?
Or am I managing my energy? And which would
benefit me more?

90.

KNOWING YOUR PURPOSE IS CRITICAL. ALIGNING YOUR
PURPOSE WITH YOUR COMPANY'S PURPOSE IS MAGICAL.

....

....

....

....

....

....

....

....

....

....

....

....

Emotional ownership is something that happens when
your purpose is aligned with your company's purpose.
That way, if the organization walks in its purpose, and
you do, you move together. You win together. Powerful
stuff. Have you experienced emotional ownership?
How can you make that a reality?

91.

KNOW AS MUCH AS YOU CAN ABOUT YOUR BUSINESS. Learn how your business is structured, and how the different parts of your business work together. It can only make you more effective.

....

....

....

....

....

....

....

....

....

....

....

....

....

....

....

92.

POWERFUL CULTURES ARE INSPIRING. Anyone who has embraced a powerful culture can be an effective contributor to yours.

....

....

....

....

....

....

....

....

....

....

In the middle of my year of learning, I visited the United States Military Academy at West Point and was amazed by their powerful military culture. It was a memorable experience. What powerful cultures have you experienced? What did you learn from them? How can you be someone who contributes to the creation of a powerful, positive culture?

93.

THOSE WHO KNOW HOW TO LISTEN, WIN.

....

....

....

....

....

....

....

94.

FOCUSING ON WHAT YOU (OR YOUR TEAM MEMBERS)
ARE GOOD AT IS ONE SURE WAY TO FIND GREAT SUCCESS.

....

....

....

....

....

....

....

95.

SLEEP IS NOT THE ENEMY.

....
....
....
....
....
....
....
....
....
....
....
....

As you work hard to accomplish your goals, how are you making sure to also rest and rejuvenate?

96.

THERE IS KINDNESS IN CANDOR.

....

....

....

....

....

....

....

....

....

....

Difficult conversations should not be about you and how you feel. They should focus on delivering the important information in a direct way, as that is kinder than beating around the bush or muddling the message. Do you know how to deliver a difficult message effectively? If not, how can you add that skill to your toolbelt?

97.

TEAM BUILDING IS NOT JUST A GAME. Delivering results through a team is sometimes the best and most effective way.

....

....

....

....

....

....

98.

CULTURE IS THE MOST POWERFUL CONTEXT WITHIN WHICH A HUMAN CAN GROW.

....

....

....

....

....

....

....

99.

IF YOU TAKE RESPONSIBILITY FOR DEFINING
WHAT "GOOD" LOOKS LIKE, YOU MAY JUST BE
ABLE TO CULTIVATE THAT GOOD ALL AROUND YOU.

100.

KNOWING "HOW THINGS GET DONE AROUND HERE"
CAN SAVE YOU ENORMOUS AMOUNTS OF TIME.

....

....

....

....

....

....

....

....

....

....

....

Walking into a new environment can be daunting.
Figure out who can help you determine the language
of that environment; learning the relevant rituals and
routines can be invaluable. Who can be your translator
in a new environment? Your coach? How can you do
a better job of learning "how things get done around
here" so you can increase your impact?

101.

YOU CAN LEARN SOMETHING VALUABLE, EVEN IF IT IS
DESCRIBED USING EXAMPLES YOU KNOW NOTHING ABOUT.

....

....

....

....

....

....

....

....

....

....

....

There are so many ways to learn. Step out of your
comfort zone when you read a book or take a course.
You may know nothing about a topic, and still learn
from reading about it. What is a new source or topic
that you can explore to expand your learning horizons?

102.

FRIENDS AND COLLEAGUES WHO ARE EXPERTS IN A SUBJECT AREA CAN BE TEACHERS JUST AS MUCH AS A COURSE, AN ARTICLE, OR A PODCAST CAN BE. Share your knowledge so someday you can be the beneficiary of someone else's.

....

....

....

....

....

....

....

....

....

....

....

....

....

....

103.

SOMETIMES IT'S SEVEN MINUTES, SOMETIMES IT'S SEVEN HOURS. IT ALL COUNTS.

....

....

....

....

....

....

....

....

....

....

....

The length of time you spend learning may or may not be related to the amount of impact you receive during your learning time—or from a specific learning source. Every minute counts. What have you learned today?

104.

AUTHENTIC NETWORKING CAN GET YOU FAR.

....

....

....

....

....

....

....

105.

DON'T TALK SO MUCH. FOCUS ON LISTENING.

....

....

....

....

....

....

....

106.

WHEN DAYS AND TO-DO LISTS GET LONG, IT IS EASY TO DECIDE THAT SPENDING TIME TO LEARN IS NOT A PRIORITY. MAKING THAT DECISION CAN LIMIT YOU.

....

....

....

....

....

....

107.

ALIGNING YOUR TIME WITH YOUR PRIORITIES IS NOT EASY, BUT ANYONE WHO IS TRULY POWERFUL IS DOING IT EVERY DAY.

....

....

....

....

....

....

108.

VERY FEW PEOPLE ARE GOOD AT DELEGATING. LEARN FROM THOSE WHO HAVE FIGURED IT OUT.

....

....

....

....

....

....

....

109.

BE A BOSS. ACHIEVE MORE BY DOING LESS. (Thanks Tiffany Dufu!)

....

....

....

....

....

....

....

110.

EVERYONE SHOULD HAVE A FEW TRUSTED SOURCES OF LEARNING.

....

....

....

....

....

....

....

111.

THE ONE WHO CAN FOCUS IS THE ONE WHO WILL WIN.

....

....

....

....

....

....

112.

EVERYONE IS SUFFERING FROM TOO MANY MINDLESS MEETINGS. BE A HERO AND CANCEL THE ONES YOU CONTROL.

....

....

....

....

....

....

113.

LOW-VALUE WORK CAN BE SEDUCTIVE. Resist! Focus on deep work and watch your impact increase.

....

....

....

....

....

....

114.

KNOWING WHEN TO WORK WITH OTHERS AND WHEN
TO WORK ALONE IS IMPORTANT.

....
....
....
....
....
....
....

115.

TRUST IS THE BOTTOM LINE.

....
....
....
....
....
....

116.

DORIE CLARK AND TODD DEWETT ARE THE BEST.

....

....

....

....

....

....

....

....

....

....

As my year of learning continued, I found that I was taking several LinkedIn Learning courses from these two thought leaders (I took a dozen from Todd!). As I assembled my trusted sources of learning, these two always delivered. Who are the thought leaders and teachers that you enjoy learning from?

117.

INSPIRE YOURSELF SO YOU CAN INSPIRE OTHERS.

....
....
....
....
....
....
....

118.

STORMS REQUIRE PATIENCE.

....
....
....
....
....
....

119.

BE RESULTS ORIENTED, RATHER THAN EFFORT ORIENTED.
It's easy to focus on "doing stuff" rather than "delivering results."
Whenever you forget, remind yourself, refocus, and execute.

120.

THE PEOPLE WHO TRULY TEACH YOU SOMETHING CAN CHANGE YOUR LIFE. If you are lucky enough to truly teach someone something, you will never really be forgotten.

....

....

....

....

....

....

....

....

....

....

....

....

Think of one of the most important things you have ever learned. Who taught you that thing?

121.

INDUSTRY REPORTS AND RESEARCH CAN PROVIDE VALUABLE INFORMATION. Find a few sources that you trust and dig in when they become available.

....

....

....

....

....

....

....

....

....

....

....

What is your go-to expert source related to the work that you do? Why do you appreciate it?

122.

CREATE A CULTURE WHERE PEOPLE FEEL EMPOWERED
TO FEARLESSLY TACKLE THEIR TASKS AND CHALLENGES,
SO THEY CAN DELIVER.

....

....

....

....

....

....

123.

HABITS HELP.

....

....

....

....

....

....

124.

HEALTH IS WEALTH. Without health and wellness, nothing else matters.

....
....
....
....
....
....
....
....
....
....
....

What are you doing to maintain and improve your health? What do you need to do and what is preventing you from doing it?

125.

IF CHANGE IS THE ONLY CONSTANT,
EMBRACING CHANGE IS WISE.

....

....

....

....

....

....

126.

PERIODICALLY, CHECK IN WITH YOURSELF AND YOUR TEAM.
ASK, "HOW ARE THINGS GOING?"

....

....

....

....

....

....

127.

SHAKING UP THE "HOW" YOU LEARN IS IMPORTANT. Sometimes it will be a success. Sometimes not so much. It is all important data.

....

....

....

....

....

....

....

128.

IF YOU ARE COMMITTED TO ACCELERATING YOUR LEARNING CURVE, LEARNING HOW YOU LIKE TO LEARN IS IMPORTANT.

....

....

....

....

....

....

....

129.

A GREAT TIME TO LEARN? WHEN YOU ARE IN A PLANE, A TRAIN, OR AN AUTOMOBILE. Turning your commute into a classroom can be a great idea.

....

....

....

....

....

....

130.

THERE ARE MANY EFFECTIVE WAYS TO CULTIVATE INFLUENCE WITHOUT AUTHORITY.

....

....

....

....

....

....

....

131.

IF THE FOUNDER OR LEADER OF YOUR COMPANY HAS
WRITTEN A BOOK, READ IT. YOU MAY FIND IT FASCINATING.

....

....

....

....

....

....

....

132.

TREAT ISSUES COLDLY, BUT TREAT PEOPLE WARMLY.

....

....

....

....

....

....

....

133.

THERE ARE SO MANY WAYS TO ENJOY *PHILLY*® CREAM CHEESE.

....

....

....

....

....

....

....

....

....

....

....

....

....

You may love something and know many ways to enjoy that thing that you love, but there are always more ways. What are some things that you love that you should commit to learn more about?

134.

FEEDBACK AND APPRAISALS WILL TELL YOU WHERE
TO FOCUS YOUR LEARNING.

....

....

....

....

....

....

135.

YOU CAN LEARN A LOT FROM A CHAT
OVER A CUP OF COFFEE.

....

....

....

....

....

....

136.

CELEBRATE ALONG THE WAY.

....

....

....

....

....

....

....

....

....

....

....

When you go on a journey, be sure to celebrate all the mile markers, milestones, and rest stops, and notice the cool scenery along the way. If your friends join you, it gets even better!

137.

THE PEOPLE WHOSE EYES LIGHT UP WHEN THEY TALK ABOUT
SOMETHING THEY HAVE LEARNED OR WANT TO LEARN?
THOSE ARE MY PEOPLE.

....

....

....

....

....

....

....

....

....

....

....

....

Who are your people?

138.

DOING GREAT THINGS CAN BE HARD.
DO GREAT THINGS ANYWAY.

....

....

....

....

....

....

139.

TRULY MEASURING YOUR IMPACT IS DIFFICULT.
FOCUS ON THE WORK, AND YOU WILL SEE IMPACT.

....

....

....

....

....

....

140.

THERE IS A LESSON IN A PEDICURE.

....

....

....

....

....

....

....

....

....

....

....

....

There are lessons in everything. As you become an
expert learner, you will see them. What is the most
unexpected place that you learned something that
ended up being important for you to know?

141.

MAKE TIME TO FOCUS ON THE UNFAMILIAR. The superpower of a lifelong learner is the ability to take any information, any experience, any challenge, and ask the question: "What can I learn from this to help me to do better, be better, achieve more?"

....

....

....

....

....

....

....

....

....

....

....

....

....

....

....

....

142.

COLD SHOWERS LEAD TO FEWER SICK DAYS.

....

....

....

....

....

....

....

....

....

....

....

....

True story. Ask the Harvard Business Review.
Do you believe it?

143.

LEARN FROM OTHER PEOPLE'S SUCCESSES AND FAILURES,
AS WELL AS YOUR OWN.

....

....

....

....

....

....

144.

THERE IS POWER IN REPETITION.

....

....

....

....

....

....

145.

HISTORY IS A GREAT TEACHER.
SO IS CONTEMPLATING THE FUTURE.

....

....

....

....

....

....

146.

CONTINUOUSLY CULTIVATING KNOWLEDGE
OF SELF IS ESSENTIAL.

....

....

....

....

....

....

147.

YOU CAN LEARN A LOT FROM PEOPLE WHO MASTER THEIR CRAFT THROUGH DILIGENCE, PRACTICE, AND MAINTAINING HIGH STANDARDS, ESPECIALLY WHEN THEY START WITH RAW TALENT.

....

....

....

....

....

....

....

....

....

....

....

....

....

....

....

148.

IF YOU ARE A LEADER, PEOPLE MANAGER, TRUSTED PEER, OR FRIEND, THE TIME MAY COME WHEN SOMEONE ASKS YOU FOR COACHING, MENTORING, AND/OR ADVICE. LEARN HOW TO GIVE IT AND RECEIVE IT.

....

....

....

....

....

....

....

....

....

....

....

....

Who is the person in your life that gives you the most valuable feedback? What do you appreciate about their feedback-giving style?

149.

PICK THE RIGHT CONFERENCE. Have a blast. Learn. Get inspired. Meet cool people.

....

....

....

....

....

....

....

150.

PEOPLE SEE, PEOPLE DO. Think critically about what you want to model—as a leader, as an expert in your field, or as a human.

....

....

....

....

....

....

....

151.

WHEN YOU LEARN, YOU INFLUENCE.

....

....

....

....

....

....

....

152.

HARNESS THE POWER OF SIMPLE.

....

....

....

....

....

....

153.

WHEN MY MOM SAID, "BLOOM WHERE YOU ARE PLANTED,"
SHE WAS RIGHT.

....

....

....

....

....

....

....

....

....

....

Dr. Patricia M. Bassey has always been a force of nature in my life. A wise woman. This is one of her favorite phrases, and I saw it time and time again in the learning materials I consumed in my year of learning. Wherever you are, always endeavor to learn and grow in that place. Especially if it is a difficult time. What do you need to learn from what you are going through today? How can you bloom where you are planted?

154.

YOU MAY BE AN EXPERT ON SOMETHING. YOU STILL CAN
ALWAYS LEARN MORE ABOUT THAT SOMETHING.

....

....

....

....

....

....

....

155.

THE IDEA OF FOCUSING ON A CUSTOMER'S "JOBS TO BE
DONE" IS FASCINATING. Solve someone's problems, and they
will be grateful.

....

....

....

....

....

....

156.

LEARN MORE ABOUT HOW HUMAN INTELLIGENCE PLUS
ARTIFICIAL INTELLIGENCE CAN MAKE UP COLLABORATIVE
INTELLIGENCE.

....

....

....

....

....

....

....

....

AI is fascinating, but check this out: The Harvard
Business Review article, "Collaborative Intelligence:
Humans and AI are Joining Forces" stated, "Through
such collaborative intelligence, humans and AI actively
enhance each other's complementary strengths:
the leadership, teamwork, creativity, and social skills
of the former, and the speed, scalability, and quantitative
capabilities of the latter." How can you make the
people and the technology in your life work together
more effectively?

157.

REST OR ACT. Spinning your wheels wastes time and energy.

....

....

....

....

....

....

....

158.

RELATIONSHIPS ARE EVERYTHING. The worst time to reach out to someone for the first time is when you need something. Learn how to create and nurture professional relationships.

....

....

....

....

....

....

159.

A GREAT MENTOR CAN MAKE A HUGE DIFFERENCE
IN YOUR LIFE. A SPONSOR CAN TRANSFORM IT.

....

....

....

....

....

....

....

....

....

....

....

....

Do you have great mentors and sponsors in your life?
If you don't yet, what can you do to find them?

160.

HALFWAY THROUGH A LONG RACE, IT IS UNDERSTANDABLE IF YOU GET TIRED. JUST KEEP RUNNING.

....

....

....

....

....

....

....

161.

IF YOU ARE STUCK TRYING TO SOLVE A PROBLEM, REFRAMING IS KEY. Ask yourself, "Am I solving the right problem?"

....

....

....

....

....

....

....

162.

LEADERSHIP IS MULTI-DIMENSIONAL.

....
....
....
....
....
....
....

163.

IF YOU ARE TRYING TO GROW LEADERS, EXPOSE THEM
TO OTHER LEADERS.

....
....
....
....
....
....
....

164.

BECOMING A LEARNED OPTIMIST IS POSSIBLE.
PRACTICE OPTIMISM.

....

....

....

....

....

....

165.

A COHORT IS POWERFUL. Having people around you to support
and encourage you can make the difference. If you are gearing up
to do a difficult thing, you may need to Squad Up!

....

....

....

....

....

....

166.

KNOWING HOW TO DEFINE 'THE AUTHENTIC YOU' CAN
HELP YOU TO BECOME THAT PERSON.

....

....

....

....

....

....

....

167.

DEVELOPING BUSINESS ACUMEN IS A
CAREER LONG ENDEAVOR.

....

....

....

....

....

....

....

168.

SUPPORTIVE COLLEAGUES ARE EVERYTHING. KNOW WHO
YOUR ALLIES ARE. TREAT THEM WELL.

....

....

....

....

....

....

....

169.

THERE ARE PEOPLE OUT THERE EVERYWHERE DYING FOR
A PAYCHECK. Guard your health as you pursue your professional
goals and aspirations.

....

....

....

....

....

....

170.

IF YOU ARE NOT PAYING FOR THE SERVICE, YOU ARE THE SERVICE. Be knowledgeable about your digital footprint.

....

....

....

....

....

....

171.

EQUITY MATTERS. Whether it is referring to fairness in everyday dealings, or providing people with ownership in their destiny, equity is important.

....

....

....

....

....

....

172.

THERE IS ALWAYS A STORY BEHIND
THE STORY. DIG DEEP TO UNDERSTAND.

....

....

....

....

....

....

....

173.

IF YOU WANT TO BE AN EFFECTIVE LEADER, REMEMBER THESE
IMPORTANT THINGS: Stop multi-tasking. Stop interrupting. Stop
trying to fix the situation. Stop discounting. Stop hogging the air.
—Marlene Chism

....

....

....

....

....

....

174.

MEASURING THE AMOUNT OF GRIT YOU ACTUALLY HAVE CAN BE A HUMBLING EXPERIENCE.

....

....

....

....

....

....

175.

DO YOUR BEST TO REMOVE THE OBSTACLES THAT CAN PREVENT YOU AND YOUR ORGANIZATION FROM LEARNING EFFECTIVELY.

....

....

....

....

....

....

176.

DIGITAL DISTRACTION IS HERE TO STAY.
FIND A WAY TO MANAGE IT.

....

....

....

....

....

....

177.

SPENDING MORE TIME IN NATURE IS IMPORTANT.

....

....

....

....

....

....

....

178.

LIVE LONG ENOUGH AND YOU WILL HAVE TO DELIVER SOME
BAD NEWS...BETTER LEARN HOW TO DO IT EFFECTIVELY.

....

....

....

....

....

....

....

179.

YOU HAVE A CHOICE – TO MULTIPLY OR DIMINISH.
WHICH WILL IT BE?

....

....

....

....

....

....

....

180.

CONNECTING PEOPLE TO THEIR PURPOSE CAN
INCREASE ENGAGEMENT.

....

....

....

....

....

....

181.

SOMETIMES IT'S WORTH REMEMBERING THAT A PICTURE
IS WORTH A THOUSAND WORDS.

....

....

....

....

....

....

182.

IT'S SIMPLE: DO THE WORK.

....

....

....

....

....

....

183.

ONE STEP AT A TIME IS OFTEN THE BEST PACE.
ESPECIALLY WHEN THINGS ARE HARD.

....

....

....

....

....

....

184.

FEEDBACK CAN BE A GIFT.

....

....

....

....

....

....

185.

INTERRUPTING YOUR ROUTINE CAN LEAD TO INNOVATION.

....

....

....

....

....

....

186.

THERE ARE A LOT OF WAYS TO GET THINGS DONE.
FIGURE OUT THE WAY THAT WORKS FOR YOU.

....

....

....

....

....

....

187.

CULTURE CHANGE CAN TACKLE THE MOST DIFFICULT
BUSINESS CHALLENGES.

....

....

....

....

....

....

188.

PEOPLE ARE OUR GREATEST ASSET; GREAT MANAGERS FIGURE OUT HOW TO REWARD THEIR TEAMS.

....

....

....

....

....

....

....

189.

SUCCESS NOW DEPENDS ON BUSINESSES BEING TOTAL LEARNING ORGANIZATIONS.

....

....

....

....

....

....

....

190.

LIFELONG LEARNING IS THE NEW LIFELINE
FOR BUSINESS SURVIVAL AND SUCCESS.

....

....

....

....

....

....

....

191.

STORIES SELL. LEARN HOW TO BE A GREAT STORYTELLER.

....

....

....

....

....

....

....

192.

**TRANSFORMATION HAPPENS,
ONE STEP AT A TIME.**

....

....

....

....

....

....

193.

**FIND OUT WHAT STANDS BETWEEN YOU AND CREATIVITY.
THEN LEARN HOW TO ELIMINATE IT.**

....

....

....

....

....

....

194.

STOP DOUBLING DOWN ON YOUR FAILING STRATEGY.

....

....

....

....

....

....

....

....

....

....

....

If you are failing, then perhaps you should consider changing your approach. This can be hard to do if you have spent time and energy going down a road. What is the best way for you to cut your losses and take another path?

195.

THERE IS A DIFFERENCE BETWEEN INNOVATION
AND IMPROVEMENT.

....

....

....

....

....

....

196.

LET YOUR PEERS INSPIRE YOU.

....

....

....

....

....

....

197.

NO MATTER WHAT YOU DO, YOU CAN LEARN SOMETHING
FROM YOUR COLLEAGUES IN MARKETING.

....

....

....

....

....

....

....

....

....

....

....

....

We are all marketing something. What can you learn
from marketing professionals about how to get and
keep a person's attention?

198.

THERE IS A VERY SPECIFIC DIFFERENCE BETWEEN STATING
YOUR VALUES AND LIVING YOUR VALUES.

....

....

....

....

....

....

....

199.

DIVERSITY IS A FACT. INCLUSION IS A CHOICE. BELONGING IS
AN OUTCOME. EQUITY IS THE GOAL.

....

....

....

....

....

....

....

200.

EVERYONE, EVERYWHERE HAS A PART TO PLAY IN EMBRACING
DIVERSITY AND MAKING THE WORLD MORE INCLUSIVE.

....

....

....

....

....

....

201.

PODCASTS CAN BE FUN. Learn with your ears instead of your eyes!

....

....

....

....

....

....

....

202.

THERE ARE SO MANY DIFFERENT WAYS TO DO SOMETHING WELL. Pick a framework that works for you, and commit to it.

....

....

....

....

....

....

203.

PLENTY OF LEARNING CAN BE ACCOMPLISHED DURING A LUNCH AND LEARN.

....

....

....

....

....

....

....

204.

LEARN WHAT AN HR BUSINESS PARTNER DOES
AND SHOULD DO.

....

....

....

....

....

....

....

....

....

....

....

....

If you are fortunate enough to work in an organization with a strong HR department, use your HR business partner to point you in the direction of the best training and learning opportunities that exist for you in your company.

205.

A FIRESIDE CHAT IS ALWAYS AWESOME, EVEN IF THERE IS NO FIRE.

....

....

....

....

....

....

206.

DIGITAL LEARNING CAN BE DELIGHTFUL.

....

....

....

....

....

....

....

207.

WHEN A FACILITATOR IS CAPTIVATING, TIME FLIES.

....

....

....

....

....

....

208.

BORING LEARNING IS A TRAGEDY. No matter what the topic, there is someone who can make it come to life. Find that person. There is no need for learning to feel like punishment.

....

....

....

....

....

....

209.

SELF-STUDY CAN BE IMPACTFUL. LEARNING WITH OTHERS CAN BE FUN. Try both, see what you like!

....

....

....

....

....

....

210.

LEARNING HOW TO TAKE A BREAK IS ALSO IMPORTANT TO LEARN.

....

....

....

....

....

....

211.

WHEN YOU LEARN SOMETHING, FIND SOMEONE WHO
CARES AND SHARE IT.

....

....

....

....

....

....

....

212.

IF YOU DON'T UNDERSTAND IT, READ IT AGAIN, CONSIDER
IT AGAIN, ASK QUESTIONS. LEARN IT UNTIL YOU GET IT.

....

....

....

....

....

....

....

213.

LOOK FOR CONNECTIONS.

....

....

....

....

....

....

....

....

....

....

....

One of the most valuable learning experiences occurs when you are presented with a topic that seems unrelated to your particular challenge or responsibility but, upon closer inspection, you realize you can learn something that will help you think creatively about something that matters to you. Have you identified a connection like that lately?

214.

WITH PRACTICE, YOU CAN BECOME A BETTER LEARNER.

....

....

....

....

....

....

....

215.

EFFECTIVE LEARNING EXPERIENCES ARE RARELY DAYS PACKED
FULL OF CONTENT. IT IS A GIFT TO BE GIVEN TIME TO BREATHE,
PROCESS, CONSIDER.

....

....

....

....

....

....

216.

COMMUNITY CAN BE POWERFUL.

....

....

....

....

....

....

217.

"ONLY THREE THINGS HAPPEN NATURALLY IN ORGANIZATIONS:
FRICTION, CONFUSION AND UNDERPERFORMANCE.
EVERYTHING ELSE REQUIRES LEADERSHIP." —PETER DRUCKER

....

....

....

....

....

....

218.

LAUGHTER MAKES LEARNING BETTER. Heck, it makes everything better!

....

....

....

....

....

....

219.

DON'T FEEL BADLY IF YOU ONLY READ PART OF A BOOK. JUST COME BACK TO IT LATER, AS YOU CAN.

....

....

....

....

....

....

220.

LEARNING WITH FRIENDS IS FUN.

....

....

....

....

....

....

....

221.

IT'S OKAY TO BE ALLERGIC TO TERRIBLE ONLINE LEARNING.
All online learning is not terrible, despite what you may have
experienced in the past. Find interactive online learning that
piques your curiosity. It's out there. I promise.

....

....

....

....

....

....

222.

NEVER STOP ASKING QUESTIONS.

....

....

....

....

....

....

223.

REMAIN CURIOUS ABOUT THE BEST
WAY FORWARD.

....

....

....

....

....

....

224.

KNOW YOUR SUPERPOWER AND KNOW YOUR KRYPTONITE.
What gives you energy? What drains it? Know both, so you can
create an environment in which you can flourish.

....
....
....
....
....
....

225.

BEFORE WORRYING ABOUT HOW TO CHANGE, FIGURE OUT
WHAT TO CHANGE.

....
....
....
....
....
....

226.

CHOOSE YOUR BATTLES WISELY.

....

....

....

....

....

....

227.

THE TRIGGER FOR ANY CORPORATE TRANSFORMATION
IS THE PURSUIT OF VALUE.

....

....

....

....

....

....

228.

BUILD WORK RELATIONSHIPS. THEY MATTER.

....

....

....

....

....

....

....

229.

MANAGE YOUR EMOTIONS WHILE NEGOTIATING.

....

....

....

....

....

....

....

230.

EXAMINE YOUR COMMUNICATIONS OFTEN. MAKE SURE THEY ARE LANDING THE WAY YOU THINK THEY ARE.

....

....

....

....

....

....

231.

GREAT LEADERS ARE COLLABORATORS.

....

....

....

....

....

....

....

232.

DIVERSITY, INCLUSION, AND BELONGING MAKES EVERY
BUSINESS PLACE A BETTER PLACE.

....

....

....

....

....

....

233.

IT IS NEVER A BAD IDEA TO FIND NEW WAYS TO
PRESENT EFFECTIVELY.

....

....

....

....

....

....

234.

THERE IS A SCIENCE TO GIVING GREAT PEP TALKS.

....

....

....

....

....

....

235.

SOMETIMES IT IS WORTHWHILE TO REVISIT THE BASICS.

....

....

....

....

....

....

236.

LEADING WITH HEART CAN TRANSFORM A CULTURE.

....

....

....

....

....

....

....

237.

THERE IS POWER IN LIVING YOUR
VALUES WILDLY.

....

....

....

....

....

....

238.

HOW YOU GATHER, MANAGE, AND USE INFORMATION WILL
DETERMINE WHETHER YOU WIN OR LOSE.

....

....

....

....

....

....

....

239.

BE INTENTIONAL AS YOU USE OR
GROW YOUR NETWORK.

....

....

....

....

....

....

240.

LEARN FROM COURSES AND FROM PEOPLE.

....

....

....

....

....

....

....

241.

A GOOD CONVERSATION CAN CHANGE YOUR PERSPECTIVE.

....

....

....

....

....

....

242.

USE YOUR NETWORK TO HELP YOURSELF AND OTHERS.

....

....

....

....

....

....

....

243.

CHANGE HEARTS AND MINDS WITH GREAT STORYTELLING.

....

....

....

....

....

....

....

244.

SOMETIMES IT TAKES SOME INSPIRATION TO CREATE
A GREAT BUDGET.

....

....

....

....

....

....

245.

CREATING A LEARNING CULTURE
TAKES TIME AND INTENTION.

....

....

....

....

....

....

246.

PEOPLE MATTER AS MUCH AS, IF NOT MORE THAN, TECHNOLOGY.

....

....

....

....

....

....

247.

ASK FOR HELP IF YOU NEED IT. AND IF YOU DON'T KNOW
HOW TO ASK, LEARN.

....

....

....

....

....

....

....

248.

MORE LEARNING IS GOOD.

....

....

....

....

....

....

249.

BE A NIMBLE LEADER. LEARN WHEN TO BE AN
ENTREPRENEURIAL LEADER, WHEN TO BE AN ENABLING
LEADER, AND WHEN TO BE AN ARCHITECTING LEADER.

....

....

....

....

....

....

250.

COMPLIANCE KEEPS THE LIGHTS ON. LEARN
HOW TO DO THE RIGHT THING.

....

....

....

....

....

....

....

251.

WHEN YOU ARE TRYING TO MAKE A SALE, MANAGE YOUR
CUSTOMER'S OBJECTIONS.

....

....

....

....

....

....

....

252.

OUTSMART THE POWER PARADOX BY PRACTICING THE ETHICS
OF EMPATHY, GRATITUDE, AND GENEROSITY.

....

....

....

....

....

....

....

253.

BRING OUT THE BEST WORK AND COLLABORATIVE SPIRIT
OF THOSE AROUND YOU.

....

....

....

....

....

....

....

254.

AS A LEADER, AIM TO EXPERIENCE THE DOPAMINE-RICH
DELIGHTS OF ADVANCING THE INTERESTS OF OTHERS.

....

....

....

....

....

....

255.

TO SUCCEED, BUILD A WORK ENVIRONMENT THAT ALIGNS
WITH UNCERTAINTY AND EMBRACES CRISIS.

....

....

....

....

....

....

256.

CHAOS CAN BE YOUR PLAYMATE.

....

....

....

....

....

....

257.

CREATE AN ATMOSPHERE FOR THE FREE EXCHANGE OF
INTELLIGENCE, UNCONSTRAINED BY FUNCTIONS AND TURF.

....

....

....

....

....

....

258.

ADVOCATE A CULTURE OF CRITICAL THINKING AND
TRANSPARENCY, AND LET THE RESULTS BE SHARED
ACCOMPLISHMENTS.

....

....

....

....

....

....

259.

VIEW STRATEGY AND EXECUTION AS A CONTINUUM,
WITH NO CLEAR BEGINNINGS OR ENDINGS.

....

....

....

....

....

....

....

260.

CRISIS DOESN'T HAVE TO BE A BAD WORD. SOMETIMES
A CRISIS CAN BE AN OPPORTUNITY.

....

....

....

....

....

....

....

261.

FIND OUT HOW INNOVATION WORKS IN YOUR
ORGANIZATION.

....

....

....

....

....

....

262.

SOMETIMES WE NEED TO BE REMINDED HOW TO BE RESILIENT.

....

....

....

....

....

....

....

263.

LEADERS EAT LAST. This is the name of a Simon Sinek book, and a brilliant lesson. Read everything from Simon Sinek, it's all delicious.

....

....

....

....

....

....

264.

SOMETIMES YOU CAN BE MORE PRODUCTIVE IF YOU INCLUDE TIME IN YOUR SCHEDULE TO BE UNPRODUCTIVE.

....

....

....

....

....

....

265.

A STRONG COMPANY CULTURE CAN IMPACT THE COMPANY'S BOTTOM LINE.

....

....

....

....

....

....

266.

IF THERE IS A GIANT ELEPHANT IN THE
ROOM, ACKNOWLEDGE IT.

....

....

....

....

....

....

....

267.

RESILIENCE IS NOT SOMETHING WE HAVE A FIXED AMOUNT
OF BUT IS SOMETHING WE CAN BUILD.

....

....

....

....

....

....

268.

DON'T VOLUNTEER TO HELP YOUR COWORKERS.

....

....

....

....

....

....

....

....

....

Interesting research that I read in Harvard Business Review: "Russell Johnson of Michigan State University and his coresearchers asked managers to track the help they gave colleagues over 10 days and how recipients responded. The team found that when people lent a hand without being asked, they were less likely to be shown gratitude than when they helped upon request. Study participants also felt less sociable and engaged at work a day after they'd given proactive assistance. The conclusion: You shouldn't volunteer to help your coworkers." What do you think?

269.

SWEAT THE TECHNIQUE.

....

....

....

....

....

....

....

....

....

....

I spent hours captivated by the book: Sweat The Technique by Rakim, one of the greatest hip hop lyricists of all times. In part of the book, he talks about creativity and innovation and how innovation can—and should come from—all sources. This aligns very much with being a lifelong learner, being intellectually curious, and being boldly creative. What creative technique can teach you a little about where to find inspiration for innovation?

270.

GREAT MARKETERS ARE GREAT STORYTELLERS.

....

....

....

....

....

....

271.

LEARN BEFORE YOU GO. When stepping out of your comfort
zone to explore a new environment, prepare, then go.

....

....

....

....

....

....

272.

LEARN WHAT "BRING YOUR WHOLE SELF TO WORK" MEANS TO YOU. It means different things to different people. When you know, do what you are comfortable with, or what you commit to becoming comfortable with.

....

....

....

....

....

....

273.

ENTHUSIASM GOES A LONG WAY.

....

....

....

....

....

....

....

274.

ANSWERING TOUGH QUESTIONS CAN ENHANCE A
LEARNING EXPERIENCE.

....

....

....

....

....

....

....

275.

IT IS WORTH IT TO FIND THE ROOT CAUSE OF
AN ISSUE. Ask questions, then ask more.

....

....

....

....

....

....

276.

PRIORITIZATION CAN PREVENT COLLABORATION OVERLOAD.

....

....

....

....

....

....

....

277.

DELEGATION CAN PREVENT BURNOUT.

....

....

....

....

....

....

278.

YOU CAN WIN BY TYING MISSION TO WHATEVER YOU ARE
TRYING TO ACCOMPLISH.

....
....
....
....
....
....
....

279.

SLEEPING ON IT DOESN'T ALWAYS LEAD TO BETTER DECISIONS.
Sometimes you can just choose to decide now.

....
....
....
....
....
....
....

280.

THE ONE WHO IS MOST ORGANIZED WINS.

....

....

....

....

....

....

....

281.

SUCCESSFUL REORGANIZATIONS REQUIRE
EFFECTIVE ORGANIZATION.

....

....

....

....

....

....

....

282.

THERE ARE THINGS TO BE LEARNED FROM ONLINE DATING.

....

....

....

....

....

....

....

....

....

....

....

This is true for so many reasons...but let's focus on the fact that the online dating industry and the evolution of all the apps that exist today is fascinating. What industries—new or old—can you learn more about in an effort to learn something new?

283.

THERE IS SUCH A THING AS TOO MANY PROJECTS. Simplify.

....

....

....

....

....

....

....

284.

BE DISCIPLINED ABOUT HOW YOU AND YOUR TEAM
SPEND YOUR TIME AND ENERGY.

....

....

....

....

....

....

....

285.

RESILIENCE IS ABOUT HOW YOU RECHARGE,
NOT HOW YOU ENDURE.

....

....

....

....

....

....

....

286.

LISTEN TO THE MEMBERS OF YOUR PERSONAL
BOARD OF DIRECTORS.

....

....

....

....

....

....

....

287.

DON'T STALL, TAKE ACTION.

....

....

....

....

....

....

....

288.

PERKS DON'T REALLY DRIVE PEOPLE AS MUCH AS PURPOSE DOES.

....

....

....

....

....

....

....

289.

MAKING PEACE WITH STRESS CAN LEAD TO MORE HAPPINESS.

....

....

....

....

....

....

....

290.

DON'T FEEL LIKE YOU HAVE TO BE HAPPY ALL THE TIME.

....

....

....

....

....

....

....

291.

A "REASONABLE WORK WEEK" IS A RELATIVE TERM. Decide what reasonable means to you, and then commit to working in that way.

....

....

....

....

....

....

....

292.

IF YOU ARE LUCKY, YOUR COMPANY VALUES ARE NOT JUST WORDS ON A WALL.

....

....

....

....

....

....

....

293.

FAMILY IS THE FIRST CLASSROOM.

....

....

....

....

....

....

294.

BE GRATEFUL MORE OFTEN.

....

....

....

....

....

....

295.

DO BETTER WORK.

....

....

....

....

....

....

296.

THE ROAD EXACTS A TOLL. If you travel for work, make sure to up your self-care so you can be your best on the road.

....

....

....

....

....

....

297.

PEOPLE'S NAMES MATTER. If you can't pronounce someone's name, just ask them. Then practice it. Then use it. People appreciate it.

....

....

....

....

....

....

298.

YOU CAN LEARN SOMETHING NEW IN AS LITTLE AS 15 MINUTES.

....

....

....

....

....

....

299.

TRADITIONAL CORPORATE CULTURE CAN BE A LIABILITY.
If you have a toxic culture, what can you do to improve it?

....

....

....

....

....

....

....

300.

EMPLOYEES REALLY WANT THREE THINGS: CAREER,
COMMUNITY AND CAUSE.

....

....

....

....

....

....

....

301.

FROM YOUR FIRST INTERNSHIP TO THE DAY YOU RETIRE, IF YOU MAKE A DECISION TO OWN YOUR OWN LEARNING AND DEVELOPMENT, YOU WILL WIN.

....

....

....

....

....

....

302.

YOU CAN LEARN A LOT FROM TAKING A SECOND LOOK AT MASLOW'S HIERARCHY.

....

....

....

....

....

....

303.

AUDACIOUS PURPOSE CAN BE POWERFUL FOR BUSINESS.

....

....

....

....

....

....

....

304.

TRAVEL AT A SUSTAINABLE SPEED TO AVOID BURNOUT FOR
YOURSELF AND YOUR TEAM.

....

....

....

....

....

....

....

305.

IT ALL COUNTS. Every minute you spend learning, reflecting, and applying your new knowledge in the real world is valuable.

....

....

....

....

....

....

306.

THERE IS AN ART TO LIVING THE GOOD LIFE.

....

....

....

....

....

....

307.

ITS FINE TO START BOOKS THAT YOU NEVER FINISH.

....

....

....

....

....

....

308.

TACKLE WHATEVER IT IS THAT PREVENTS YOU FROM BEING
THE PERSON YOU WANT TO BE OR DOING THE THINGS YOU
WANT TO DO.

....

....

....

....

....

....

309.

OFTEN, LEARNING IS DELIGHTFUL.

....

....

....

....

....

....

....

310.

RIDESHARES ARE GREAT PLACES TO LEARN SOMETHING NEW.

....

....

....

....

....

....

....

311.

NAVY SEALS KNOW A THING OR TWO ABOUT OWNERSHIP.

....

....

....

....

....

....

....

312.

SOMETIMES YOU WIN, SOMETIMES YOU LOSE...BUT IF YOU ARE LUCKY, YOU LEARN SOMETHING EVERY TIME.

....

....

....

....

....

....

313.

SPENDING TIME WITH THE WORDS OF YOUR FAVORITE
AUTHOR CAN BE QUITE REJUVENATING.

....

....

....

....

....

....

314.

REMARKABLE THINGS HAPPEN WHEN
YOU DARE TO DREAM.

....

....

....

....

....

....

315.

LEADERS MUST BE LEARNING CONTINUALLY.

....

....

....

....

....

....

316.

TO BE AN INCLUSIVE LEADER, YOU MUST UNDERSTAND
INTERSECTIONALITY.

....

....

....

....

....

....

317.

YOU CAN LEARN SOME IMPORTANT LEADERSHIP LESSONS
FROM ATTILA THE HUN.

....

....

....

....

....

....

....

318.

RELAXING EFFECTIVELY IS A SKILL THAT CAN BE LEARNED.

....

....

....

....

....

....

....

319.

IT IS CRUCIAL TO LEARN HOW TO FORGET ABOUT WORK
WHEN YOU ARE NOT AT WORK.

....

....

....

....

....

....

....

320.

MASTERCLASS IS A LEARNER'S PARADISE.

....

....

....

....

....

....

....

321.

DOWNTIME MOST CERTAINLY
HAS AN UPSIDE.

....

....

....

....

....

....

322.

CHIEF LEARNING OFFICERS CAN BE AGENTS OF
TRANSFORMATION AND AMPLIFICATION.

....

....

....

....

....

....

....

323.

GET YOURSELF A TRIBE OF MENTORS.

....

....

....

....

....

....

....

324.

THERE IS A TED TALK FOR EVERY SITUATION TO PROVIDE
WHATEVER INSPIRATION YOU NEED.

....

....

....

....

....

....

....

325.

THERE ARE SMALL, UNFORGETTABLE NUGGETS OF WISDOM
WITHIN EVERY ENORMOUS BOOK.

....

....

....

....

....

....

326.

IF YOU DECIDE TO #MAKETIMEFORLEARNING, THE RETURN
ON YOUR INVESTMENT WILL BE HUGE.

....

....

....

....

....

....

....

327.

STOP WORRYING ABOUT HOW MUCH YOU MATTER.

....

....

....

....

....

....

....

....

....

....

....

Sometimes the right thing to do is to focus on the work instead of people's perceptions of how you do the work. Is there a task you are working on that would worry you less if you weren't thinking about how people will feel about how you complete it?

328.

THERE IS A TIME AND A PLACE FOR STRUCTURED LEARNING.
AND, THERE IS ALSO A TIME AND A PLACE FOR INTELLECTUAL
CURIOSITY, TO COMMITTING TO A REGULAR PRACTICE OF
CONTINUOUS LEARNING. Finding interesting perspectives
that provide new ways of thinking can happen when you make
a habit of learning.

....

....

....

....

....

....

....

....

....

....

....

....

....

329.

IF YOU'VE EVER FELT STUCK, STRUGGLED WITH SELF-DOUBT,
OR WORRIED ABOUT FINDING SUCCESS, JUST FOCUS
ON THE WORK.

....

....

....

....

....

....

330.

INSPIRING LEARNERS TO LEARN IS AN ART AND A SCIENCE.

....

....

....

....

....

....

....

331.

MAKE SURE TO LEARN FROM YOUR DISASTERS
AND YOUR FAILURES.

....

....

....

....

....

....

332.

FIND WAYS TO UNLEASH THE QUIET GENIUS OF
YOUR EMPLOYEES.

....

....

....

....

....

....

333.

REAL LEADERS KNOW HOW TO HANDLE A CRISIS.

....

....

....

....

....

....

334.

A CONVERSATION WITH THE RIGHT PERSON CAN CHANGE EVERYTHING.

....

....

....

....

....

....

335.

LEADERSHIP IS A CONTACT SPORT.
GET IN THE GAME!

....

....

....

....

....

....

336.

GREAT LEADERS PRACTICE BEING SELF-AWARE.

....

....

....

....

....

....

337.

ASK YOURSELF FROM TIME TO TIME, "HOW WILL YOU
MEASURE YOUR LIFE?"

....

....

....

....

....

....

....

....

....

....

....

....

This is a thought-provoking question, posed by Clay
Christensen. Research him, he was a brilliant man.

338.

TAKING THE TIME TO CULTIVATE COURAGE IS WORTHWHILE.

....

....

....

....

....

....

339.

KNOWING WHAT MOTIVATES YOUR MANAGER CAN HELP
YOU IN YOUR CAREER.

....

....

....

....

....

....

340.

HARNESS THE POWER OF TRANSPARENCY.

....

....

....

....

....

....

....

341.

LEADERS DON'T ALWAYS HAVE THE ANSWERS.

....

....

....

....

....

....

....

342.

AMAZING LEARNING CAN COME FROM
A SIMPLE KEYWORD SEARCH.

....

....

....

....

....

....

343.

NOT EVERYONE IS AN EXPLORATORY LEARNER BY NATURE,
BUT IT'S WORTH IT TO GIVE IT A SHOT.

....

....

....

....

....

....

344.

IN SHARING WHAT YOU LEARN, YOU CAN CONTRIBUTE TO
A CULTURE OF GENEROSITY.

....

....

....

....

....

....

345.

CREATE RITUALS AND ROUTINES AROUND LEARNING.

....

....

....

....

....

....

....

346.

SOMETIMES LEARNING A THING IS SWEETER THE SECOND
TIME AROUND.

....

....

....

....

....

....

347.

SO MUCH TO LEARN, SO LITTLE TIME.

....

....

....

....

....

....

348.

LEARNING FROM PEERS—INSIDE AND OUTSIDE OF YOUR
ORGANIZATION—CAN BE VALUABLE.

....

....

....

....

....

....

....

349.

THINK OF LEARNING AS A PRIVILEGE, NOT A PUNISHMENT.

....

....

....

....

....

....

....

350.

IN EFFECTIVE COMMUNICATION, A COMBINATION OF FACTS
AND EMOTION IS WHAT INSPIRES.

....

....

....

....

....

....

....

351.

MAKE SURE YOUR TEAM FEELS VALUED AND SUPPORTED.

....

....

....

....

....

....

....

352.

COMPETENT COURAGE CAN MAKE
THE DIFFERENCE.

....

....

....

....

....

....

353.

KNOWING WHEN TO DIG IN AND WHEN TO DELEGATE IS
SOMETHING THAT TAKES PRACTICE.

....

....

....

....

....

....

354.

BEING RISK AVERSE CAN PREVENT YOU FROM BEING CREATIVE AND INNOVATIVE.

....

....

....

....

....

....

355.

NO MATTER HOW MUCH YOU EMBRACE FAILURE AS A LEARNING EXPERIENCE, IT STILL KIND OF SUCKS.

....

....

....

....

....

....

....

356.

WORK TAKES UP AS MUCH TIME AS YOU GIVE IT.
LEARN TO TIMEBOX.

....

....

....

....

....

....

....

357.

OBSERVE SUCCESSFUL, EFFECTIVE, BUSY PEOPLE. THEY CAN
TEACH YOU A LOT.

....

....

....

....

....

....

....

358.

IF YOU HAVE A STRONG NEGATIVE REACTION TO A SPEAKER
OR AN ARTICLE, TAKE NOTE. THAT IS AS USEFUL AS IF YOU
THOUGHT THE SPEAKER OR ARTICLE WAS AMAZING.

....

....

....

....

....

....

359.

IT IS SUPER COOL TO MEET SOMEONE AFTER THEY HAVE
TAUGHT YOU SO MUCH THROUGH eLEARNING.

....

....

....

....

....

....

....

360.

FOCUS NOT JUST ON BEING BUSY, BUT ON
DELIVERING RESULTS.

....

....

....

....

....

....

....

361.

WHEN YOU FIGURE OUT YOUR NARRATIVE, NEVER TIRE
OF SHARING IT.

....

....

....

....

....

....

....

362.

HAVING SUPPORTIVE LEADERSHIP IS EVERYTHING.

....

....

....

....

....

....

....

363.

"AHA" MOMENTS—THOSE MOMENTS OF SUDDEN INSIGHT
OR DISCOVERY—ARE MAGICAL.

....

....

....

....

....

....

....

Move

Move

From Curious to Competent

LESSONS 364 and 365

If you haven't already started using this section of the journal to document your own learning journey, (or even if you have), I invite you to use this part of the journal to write about how you would like to apply your learning habit going forward.

THE LAST TWO LESSONS OF THE 365 THINGS I LEARNED FROM 365 DAYS OF LEARNING WERE:

364.

IF YOU REALLY WANT TO KNOW SOMETHING, YOU WILL EVENTUALLY
HAVE TO TRAVEL THE ROAD FROM AWARENESS TO APPLICATION.

365.

MOVE FROM CURIOUS TO COMPETENT.

Learning something in a regular cadence is important. Habits are
everything. Remaining committed to trying and applying things to
see how they work in different situations is crucial.

When you are convinced of the power of a learning habit, you are
well on your way to unleashing your learning superpower. Figuring
out your unique way to move from curious to competent can help
you to grow a great career, step into your light, and embed the
lessons from your learning journey into how you live and lead.

So, what happens after a year of learning, you may wonder? For me,
in year 2, I made a commitment to complete and share 100 learning
experiences with my organization. That was challenging in a
different way than making my initial daily learning habit. In year 3,
I made a list of the different topics on which I wanted to focus my
learning time. These are the topics in which I want to make sure I
remain on the cutting edge of my competency so I can be highly
effective in my personal and professional life. What skills,
competencies, and capabilities are you focused on developing?
Use the following pages to document your thoughts as you continue
your commitment to continuous learning.

What I am Learning

Thank You

~~~~~~

Throughout *My 365 Days of Learning*, I had the pleasure of learning from so many different business and thought leaders, academics and authors, friends and colleagues. I have listed them below. Their wisdom has become part of my body of knowledge, and it influences and inspires the words of wisdom that are in this journal. Of course, the caveat is that I could never list everyone that I learned from over the span of the year. Creating an exhaustive list of teachers is an impossible task for a continuous learner. Below are those who had a hand in creating or delivering the 365 learning experiences that inspired this journal. I ask for the forgiveness of anyone I may have inadvertently omitted. To the reader, I encourage you to research these amazing folks further if your interest is piqued. As lesson #342 stated, "Amazing learning can come from a simple keyword search."

In my year of learning, I appreciate everything I learned from and through:

Abbie Lundberg	Alexandra Samuel	Amy C. Edmonson
Acha Leke	Alexi Vella	Andre Fernandez
Adam Brandenburger	Alice Wastag	Andrea Scott
Adam Grant	Alison Beard	Andrew Brodsky
Adi Ignatius	Alison Wood Brooks	Andrew G. Rundle
Alan Mulally	All Kraft Heinz	Andrew Keatings
Alan Patterson	Employees	Andrew M. Carton
Alan Siegel	Amanda N. Young	Andrew M. Rosenfield
Alessandra de Dreuille	Amanda Young	Andrew Roscoe
Alessandro Castilletti	Amy Balliett	Andy Ding
Alex Lazarus	Amy Bosek	Angela Duckworth
Alexandra Hyland	Amy Humble	Angela Lee

Angela V. Paccione
Annibal Goncalves
Art Markman
Asmita Singh
Audrey Epstein
Avinash Maharaj
Barbara Oakley
Barry Linetsky
Ben Casnocha
Bernardo Hees
Beth Comstock
Bhavya Mohan
Bill Bartlett
Bill Burnett
Bill George
Biz Stone
Black Enterprise
   Magazine
Blinkist
Bloomberg
Bob Iger
Bob Kulhan
Boris Groysberg
Bradley Staats
Brenda Bailey-Hughes
Brene Brown
Brian J. Lucas
Brien Convery
Britt Andreatta, PhD
Bruno Keller
Brynn Harrington
C.C. Chapman
Cal Newport
Carlos Abrams-Rivera
Carlos Faria
Carol Kinsey Goman
Carol Knight-Wallace
Carol Lavin Bernick
Carol Rissling
Carol S. Dweck, Ph.D.
Carol Stephenson
Caroline Boulos
Caroline Webb

Center for Talent
   Innovation
Cesar Urbina
Charles Duhigg
Chester Elton
Chief Learning Officer
   Magazine
#ChocolateCardinal
Chris Edmonds
Chris Westfall
Chris Yeh
Christiane Correa
Christine D. Bataille
Christopher Barnes
Christopher Kirchhoff
Christopher Reid
Claire Shipman
Claudio Fernandez-Araoz
Clayton M. Christensen
Colin Haddley
Colleen Boselli
Colonel Hise Gibson
Columbia Business
   School
Constance Noonan
   Hadley
Cornell University SC
Johnson Graduate
   School of Business
Corrine Armour
Craig W. Ross
Curtis Odom
Cynthia Marshall
Dacher Keltner
Dan Cable
Dan Coughlin
Daniel Kahneman
Daniel McGinn
Daniel Mochon
Daria Veprek
Dave Crenshaw
Dave Evans
Dave Ulrich

David A. Garvin
David Allen
David Bechtold
David Hoyt
David Lazer
David M. Upton
David S. Duncan
David Shaw
Dayna Rothman
Dean Carter
Deb Taylor
Deborah Ancona
Deepak Chopra
Deloitte
Delta Sigma Theta,
   Omicron Chi Chapter
Denise Lee Yohn
Dickie Lian-Hong Ke
Diwas S. KC
Donald Cooper
Donna Flynn
Dorie Clark
EBSCO
Eddie Turner
Eduardo Mayer
Ehrnberg-Bass Institute
   for Marketing Science
Elaine Backman
Elias Diaz
Elizabeth (McLeod)
   Lotardo
Elizabeth Obbard
Elizabeth Ottolini
Emilie Stanczyk
Emily Briggs
Emily McTague
Emma K. MacDonald
Emuata Bassey
Enrique de Diego
Erika Andersen
Erin Reid
Ethan Bernstein
Eunice Eun

Kim Scott
Kristie Rogers
Kyle Maynard
Laine Joelson Cohen
La June Davies-Wiley
Lakshmi Ramarajan
Lan Tran
Lance Secretan
Larry Rosen
Lawrence H. Summers
Lee Ellis
Leif Babin
Leisa Sargent
Leonard L. Berry
Lesley Owens
Leslie A. Perlow
Leslie K. John
Levi Nieminen
Lida Citroën
Lil Jon
Linda Nacif
Linda Ruffenach
Linda Sharkey
LinkedIn Learning
Linnea Gandhi
Lisa Earle McLeod
Liz M. Janz
Liz Wiseman
LLAO Learning
  Ambassadors
Lori Goler
Lori J Pisacane
Lou Patler
Luciana Iliescu
Luvvie Ajayi Jones
Lynn Freehill-Maye
MacKenzie Collins
Maeyen Bassey
Maha Ibrahim
Mandel Communications
Mandy Ginsberg
Mani Gopalakrishnan
Marcos Eloi

Marcos Tasso
Maria Konnikova
Marianne Cabrera
Marina Ashavsky
Marisa Fong
Mark Emery
Mark H. McCormack
Marla Blow
Marlene Chism
Marshall Goldsmith
Marshall Goldsmith's
  100 Coaches
Marva Sadler
Mary Dean Lee
Maryam Kouchaki
Matt Plummer
Matthew Toporski
Max Yoder
Melissa Werneck
Merete Wedell-
  Wedellsborg
Michael Alden
Michael Bungay Stanier
Michael D. Watkins
Michael Etomi
Michael F. Andrew
Michael Friedman
Michael McLernon
Michael Mullen
Michael Scissons
Michael Strahan
Michelle Gielan
Michelle Obama
Miguel Patricio
Mike Figliuolo
Mike Krzyewski
Mike Rogers
Mike Spinelli
Mory Fontanez
My Family
N. Anand
National Advisory Board,
  Haas Center for

Public Service,
  Stanford University
Nancy P. Rothbard
Naphtali Bryant
Nav Bhatia
Nicholas L. Tarleton
Nick Koors
Nick Offerman
Nick Van Dam
Nina Barton
Nir Eyal
Niro Sivanthan
Nneka Rimmer
Oliver Emrich
Olivia "Liv" Boeree,
Omar Rodriguez Vila
Ownerversity
Paradigm
Pat Lencioni
Pat Wador
Patricia Bassey
Patrick J. McKenna
Patrick Spenner
Paul Axtell
Paul Gholston
Paul R. Daugherty
Paul Smith
Paulo Basilio
Pedro Albuquerque
Peter B. Cotter
Peter Bregman
Peter Field
Peter Hall
Peter Reiss
Prakash Raman
Quentin Fottrell
Rachel Pitman
Rafael Oliveira
Rakim
Randy Kessler
Ranjay Gulati
Raphael Bozza
Rashida La Lande

Rebecca Spencer
Reid Hoffman
Rev. Dr. Martin Luther
   King, Jr.
Rich Horwath
Richard Branson
Rob Cross
Robert D. Ramsey, EdD
Robert McKee
Robin Abrahams
Robyn Scott
Rolf Dobelli
Rose Hollister
Russell Johnson
Ryan Brown
Ryan Jacoby
Ryan W. Buell
Saf Yeboah-Amankwah
Sallie Krawcheck
Sally Helgesen
Sam Shriver
Samantha Hammock
Samin Nosrat
Sankaranarayanan
   Padmanabhan
Sanket Sinha
Sanyin Siang
Sara Azofeifa
Sarah Beckham
Sarah Clayton
Sarah Higgins
Sarah Patrick
Sarang Jain
Satya Nadella
Scott Berinato
Scott Edinger
Scott Taylor
Scott W. Davis
Second City Works
Selena Cuffe
Senia Maymin
Serena Chew
Serena Huang

Serena Rahme
Seth Godin
Shane Snow
Sharon Drew Morgen
Shawn Achor
Shelly F. Hall
Sheryl Sandberg
Shirley Weinstein
Sid Mohasseb
Simon Sinek
Skyler Logsdon
Sofia Yurasova
Sonny Iqbol
Stacey Hanke
Stacey Johnson
Stanford University
   Graduate School
   of Business
Stanislov Shekshnia
State of Women of
   Color in Dallas
Stefan Mumaw
Stephane Kasriel
Stephanie Taylor
   Christensen
Stephen Covey
Stephen Gaonach
Stephen Heidari-
   Robinson
Sterling K. Brown
Steven Callander
Steven Pressfield
Steven Prokesch
Sue Hawkes
Sundar Bharadwaj
Susan Cain
Susan Newhouse
Suzanne Heywood
Suzanne M. Johnson
   Vickberg
Sydney Finkelstein
Tacy Byham
Taddy Hall

Taryn Marie Stejskal
Tasha Eurich
Tatiana Kolovou
Teresa M. Amabile
Terry Crews
The 2019 Kraft Heinz
   Leadership Masters
   cohort
The Cara Group
Thiago D. Bastos
Thomas Wedell-
   Wedellsborg
Tiffany Dufu
Timothy Ferriss
Timothy Geithner
Tiziana Casciaro
Todd Dewett
Todd S. Sherman
Tom Blaser
Tom DeCotiis
Tom Gentile
Tony Fadell
Tony Schwartz
Tracey A. Revenson
Tracy L. Dumas
Tricia Brouk
Trish Holliday
Umberto Fedelli
Valerie Purdie
   Greenaway
Victoria L Roberts
Victoria Sjardin
Vinnie Gaynor
Vlatka Hlupic
Wayne Baker
Wayne Cheneski
Wendy Sachs
Wess Roberts, PhD
Whitney Johnson
William Kerr
Yael Zofi
Yang Xu
Zander Lurie

About the Author

Ekpedeme "Pamay" M. Bassey is a lifelong learner who loves laughter, words, big ideas, and serving her community.

She is Chief Learning and Diversity Officer for the Kraft Heinz Company, where she creates an inclusive culture of continuous learning, bold creativity, and intellectual curiosity, drives the company's global training and learning strategy, programs, and initiatives, and amplifies the work that every Kraft Heinz employee does to create a diverse and inclusive workplace.

Pamay is also Chief Experience Officer of the *My 52 Weeks of Worship Project*, through which she facilitates courageous conversations about cultural and interfaith diversity, inclusion, and understanding. Her 2018 TEDx talk, *Navigating Sacred Spaces* - and the weekly journal of the same name - are both based on her project work and her book, *My 52 Weeks of Worship: Lessons from a Global, Spiritual, Interfaith Journey*.

SEVEN STEPS OF LEARNING TRANSFORMATION

1.
Embrace the
value proposition

2.
Commit to
#LearnLikeAnOwner

3.
Identify your trusted source(s)
of learning

4.
Determine your searching
and learning style

5.
Reflect on and share
what you are learning

6.
Determine what to practice
and what to keep

7.
Apply your learning habit
to something specific